Agile Discussion Guide

This guide is continually evolving as we uncover better ways of developing software by practicing and helping others practice Agile.

Subscribe to the Agile Discussion guide email list to stay up to date with the latest version

LeanDog.com/downloads

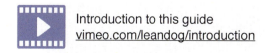

Introduction to this guide
vimeo.com/leandog/introduction

LeanDog, Inc.
1151 North Marginal Road Cleveland, Ohio 44114

All rights reserved. No part of this book may be reproduced or transmitted in any form or by any means, electronic or mechanical, including photocopying, recording or by any information storage and retrieval system, without written permission from the author, except for the inclusion of brief quotations in a review.

Copyright © 2015 by LeanDog

Table of Contents

Acknowledgement	6
Preface	7

1 Introduction to Agile — 9

Agile Manifesto	10
Principles Behind the Agile Manifesto	11
Fundamentals, Roles and Practices	12
Practices Mapped to Values	13
Agile History	14
Agile Culture & Process Case Study: IDEO	15
Oath of Non-Allegiance	16
Company Ecosystem	17
Agile Benefits Realized	18

2 Agile Concepts — 19

Agile Concepts	20
Whole Team	21
Open Workspace	22
T-Shaped People	25
Sustainable Pace	26
Information Radiators	27
Frequent Releases	29
Story Card Wall	30
Agile Triangle	32
Cone of Uncertainty	33

3 Agile Process — 35

Agile Process	36
Kanban	37
Scrum Framework	39
Story Card Writing	41
Estimation & Sizing	43
Sprints/Iterations	44
Customer Collaboration	45

4 Leadership — 47

Leadership Role	48
Servant Leadership	49
Six Thinking Hats	50
Collaboration 8	52
Fist to 5	54

5 Scrum Master / Iteration Manager — 55

Scrum Master / Iteration Manager	56
Daily Scrum/Stand Up	57
Sprint/Iteration Planning	58
Show & Tell	59
Retrospectives	60
Velocity	61
Roadblocks	62

6 Quality Assurance — 63

Quality Assurance Role	64
Exploratory Testing	65
Automated Regression Testing	66
Acceptance Test Driven Development	67

7 Developer — 71

Developer Role	72
Collective Code Ownership	73
Continuous Integration	74
Simple & Evolutionary Design	75
Paired Programming (Pairing)	76
Test Driven Development	77
Technical Debt	78
Spikes	79

8 Product Owner — 81

Product Owner Role	82
Value Stream Mapping	83
Demand Management	84
Product Backlog	85
Release Planning	86

9 User Experience — 87

User Experience Designer — 88
Personas — 89
Story Mapping — 90
Low-Fidelity Prototyping — 91

10 Appendix — 93

Recommended Reading List — 94
Additional Downloads — 97
About this Author — 98

Acknowledgement

The following folks have helped bring this guide to life by contributing content, design, filming and edits throughout the print book as well as the interactive version.

 Jon Stahl
 Jeff Morgan
 Michael Norton
 Matt Barcomb
 James Grenning

 Kathryn Guess
 Eric Hankinson
 Angela Harms
 Shane Hayes
 Joel Helbling

 Jodi Carlson
 Susan Gibson
 Dan Parks
 Nicole Capuana
 Michael Lutton

 David Shah
 Matt Fousek
 Steve Jackson
 Joel Byler
 Sahithya Wintrich

 Michael Jebber
 Matt Volosin
 Pat Kelly
 Chris Nurre
 Paul Carvahlo

Preface

This guide is a comprehensive introduction to basic Agile terminology, practices, and thinking. While we have had many customers ask us for a "checklist on Agile", every team is different and no two teams practice Agile the same way. This guide serves as a blueprint, not a roadmap. We have defined and outlined the basic principles and practices of Agile through a discussion about the practices between you and an experienced LeanDog Agile coach.

Essential vs Advanced

Each practice falls into one of two categories: essential and advanced. Essential practices are crucial to adopting Agile. Advanced practices, on the other hand, are not critical but greatly improve essential practices. Regardless of which practices you choose to adopt, we strongly suggest that this guide be used in the spirit of collaboration. As Agile is about constant improvement, it's very common to adopt the essential tasks first, and incorporate advanced tasks as you become more comfortable with Agile.

Book Legend

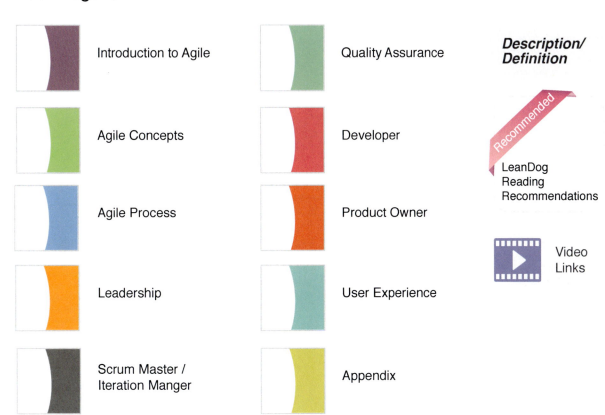

Chapter 1

Introduction to Agile

In this chapter
- Agile Manifesto
- Principles Behind the Agile Manifesto
- Agile Practices
- Practices Mapped to Agile Values
- Agile History
- Agile Culture & Process Case Study: IDEO
- Oath of Non-Allegiance
- Company Ecosystem
- Agile Benefits Realized

Agile Manifesto

We are uncovering better ways of developing software by doing it and helping others do it. Through this work we have come to value:

- **Individuals and Interactions** over Processes and Tools
- **Working Software** over Comprehensive Documentation
- **Customer Collaboration** over Contract Negotiation
- **Responding to Change** over Following a Plan

That is, while there is value in the items on the right, we value the items on the left more[1].

Agile Manifesto History

In 2001, a group of 17 people who are passionate about simple and minimalistic software practices met in Snowbird, Utah to discuss their approaches and best processes. These representatives from eXtreme Programming (XP), Scrum, DSDM, Adaptive Software Development and others "sympathetic to the need for an alternative to documentation driven, heavyweight software development process" uncovered better ways of developing software by doing it and helping others do it.

Through collaboration, the Agile Manifesto was created outlining four value statements and 12 principles. While most people only read the values, it is important that the principles are understood as well. The values define the overall objectives of the Agile methodology, making up the "WHY in Agile", while the principles define the tenets that feed into the values, becoming the "WHAT in Agile". Finally, the practices serve as the "HOW in Agile", providing the blueprint to follow [1].

The 17 Authors of the Agile Manifesto:

Kent Beck
Mike Beedle
Arie van Bennekum
Alistair Cockburn
Ward Cunningham
Martin Fowler
James Grenning
Jim Highsmith
Andrew Hunt
Ron Jeffries
Jon Kern
Brian Marick
Robert C. Martin
Steve Mellor
Ken Schwaber
Jeff Sutherland
Dave Thomas

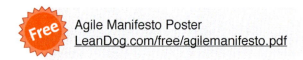
Agile Manifesto Poster
LeanDog.com/free/agilemanifesto.pdf

vimeopro.com/leandog/manifesto

1 Kent Beck, et al http://www.agilemanifesto.org

Principles Behind the Agile Manifesto

Our highest priority is to satisfy the customer through early and continuous delivery of valuable software.

Welcome changing requirements, even late in development. Agile processes harness change for the customer's competitive advantage.

Deliver working software frequently, from a couple of weeks to a couple of months, with a preference to the shorter time scale.

Business team and developers must work together daily throughout the project.

Build projects around motivated individuals. Give them the environment and support they need, and trust them to get the job done.

The most efficient and effective method of conveying information to and within a development team is face-to-face conversation.

Working software is the primary measure of progress.

Agile processes promote sustainable development. The sponsors, developers, and users should be able to maintain a constant pace indefinitely.

Continuous attention to technical excellence and good design enhances agility.

Simplicity - the art of maximizing the amount of work not done - is essential.

The best architectures, requirements, and designs emerge from self-organizing teams.

At regular intervals, the team reflects on how to become more effective, then tunes and adjusts its behavior accordingly[1].

Agile Principles Poster
LeanDog.com/free/agile-manifestoprinciples1.pdf

1 Kent Beck, et al http://www.agilemanifesto.org

Fundamentals, Roles and Practices

LeanDog created the "Fundamentals, Roles and Practices" chart below to give a vision into how the Agile Values and Principles can be leveraged.

You don't have to implement every practice, but each practice adds value. We encourage you to explore practices, try them, and evaluate them yourself. Adopting a major company change isn't always popular, and can cause discord and resistance. This chart helps ease the transition. Not only does it give a snapshot of the overall Agile methodology, but it clearly defines the practices of each craft. Once employees understand the purpose of the change, and its importance to both the company's goals and their own work responsibilities, they will be more likely to accept the change.

Roles and Practices

Fundamentals

Concepts
- Whole Team
- Open Workspace
- T-Shaped People
- Sustainable Pace
- Information Radiators
- Frequent Releases
- Story Card Wall
- Agile Triangle
- Cone of Uncertainty

Process
- Kanban
- Scrum Framework
- Story Card Writing
- Estimation & Sizing
- Sprints/Iterations
- Customer Collaboration

Leadership
- Servant Leadership
- Six Thinking Hats
- Collaboration 8
- Fist to 5

Scrum Master / Iteration Manager
- Daily Scrum/Stand Up
- Sprint/Iteration Planning
- Show & Tell
- Retrospectives
- Velocity
- Roadblocks

Quality Assurance
- Exploratory Testing
- Automated Regression Testing
- Acceptance Test Driven Development

Developer
- Collective Code Ownership
- Continuous Integration
- Simple & Evolutionary Design
- Paired Programming (Pairing)
- Test Driven Development
- Technical Debt
- Spikes

Product Owner
- Story Card Writing
- Value Stream Mapping
- Demand Management
- Product Backlog
- Release Planning

User Experience
- Personas
- Story Mapping
- Low-Fidelity Prototyping

 vimeopro.com/leandog/agilepractices

Practices Mapped to Agile Values

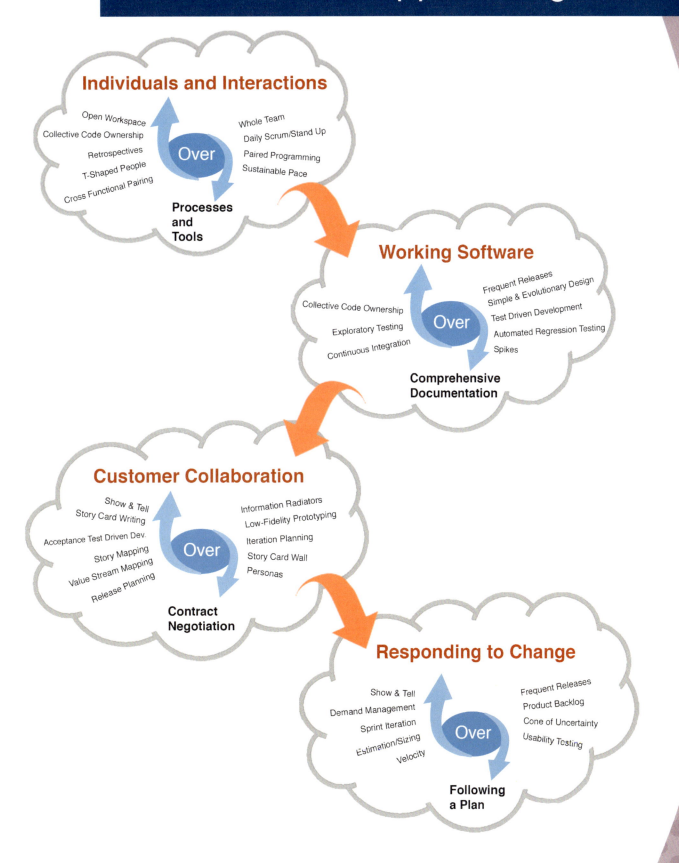

Agile History

Incremental software development methods trace back to 1957. Lightweight software development methods first appeared in the mid-1990s in reaction to the heavyweight waterfall-oriented methods that had become commonplace, which critics called heavily regulated, regimented, micromanaged and over-incremental.

Proponents of these lightweight methods contended that they were returning to development practices that were present early in the history of software. These early implementations favored creativity, freedom, self-management and continuous improvement. These methods are now collectively referred to as Agile development, after the Agile Manifesto was published in 2001.

The term "Lean" was coined to describe Toyota's Production System during the late 1980s by a research team at MIT. The core idea is to maximize customer value while minimizing waste. In the early 2000s, companies (especially startups) began applying both Lean and Agile principles together in order to develop new products (or even new companies) more efficiently and based on validated customer demand.

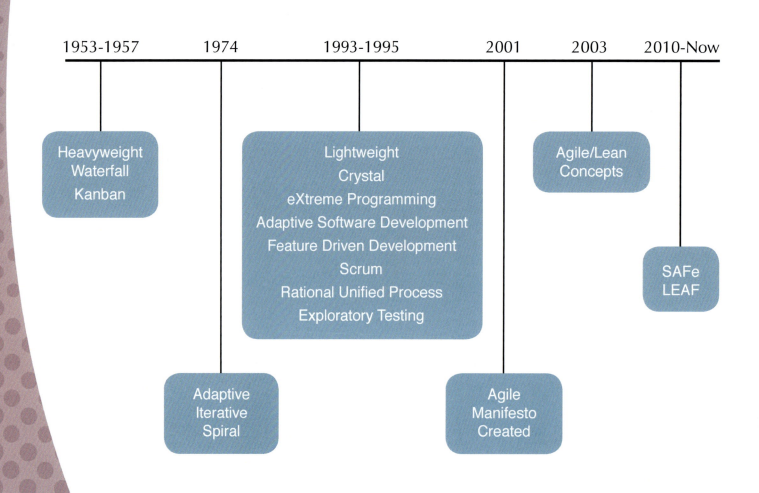

Agile Culture & Process Case Study: IDEO

The IDEO Deep Dive video on ABC Nightline is about a team at IDEO that reinvented the shopping cart in one week. While watching the video, ask yourself:
1. How does the process of designing a better product work?
2. What does a process and a culture look like?

Online at: youtube.com/watch?v=M66ZU2PCIcM [1]

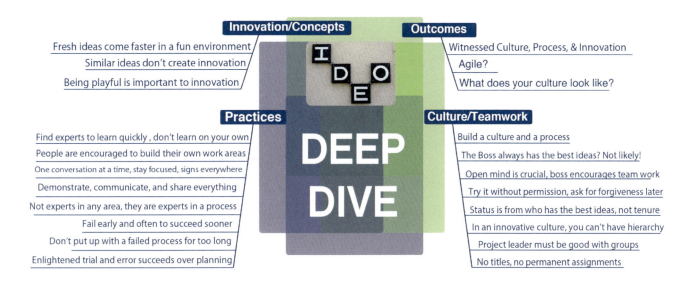

Innovation/Concepts
- Fresh ideas come faster in a fun environment
- Similar ideas don't create innovation
- Being playful is important to innovation

Outcomes
- Witnessed Culture, Process, & Innovation
- Agile?
- What does your culture look like?

Practices
- Find experts to learn quickly, don't learn on your own
- People are encouraged to build their own work areas
- One conversation at a time, stay focused, signs everywhere
- Demonstrate, communicate, and share everything
- Not experts in any area, they are experts in a process
- Fail early and often to succeed sooner
- Don't put up with a failed process for too long
- Enlightened trial and error succeeds over planning

Culture/Teamwork
- Build a culture and a process
- The Boss always has the best ideas? Not likely!
- Open mind is crucial, boss encourages team work
- Try it without permission, ask for forgiveness later
- Status is from who has the best ideas, not tenure
- In an innovative culture, you can't have hierarchy
- Project leader must be good with groups
- No titles, no permanent assignments

[1] ABC Nightline, IDEO Deep Dive, http://www.youtube.com/watch?v=M66ZU2PCIcM

Oath of Non-Allegiance

" I promise not to exclude from consideration any idea based on its source, but to consider ideas across schools and heritages in order to find the ones that best suit the current situation.[1] "

An Agile approach focuses on empowered, self-managing teams; autonomy that doesn't need day-to-day intervention by management[2]. Instead, Agile management means protecting the team from outside interference and removing roadblocks that impede the delivery of business value and productivity. It is widely accepted that complex systems cannot be predicted[3] and are best managed using empirical process controls; therefore, management allows self-managing teams to build systems in an empirical manner[4].

What Does it Mean to "Be Agile?"

Considering that Agile is a set of values and principles, becoming Agile means upholding these values and principles. It's not about doing one practice (for example Scrum) and declaring that you are Agile. Instead, it's about continually seeking better ways of delivering software. We coach your company to adopt this culture and implement practices that are based on the needs of your teams and projects.

LeanDog Signed the Oath of Non-Allegiance so should you

At LeanDog, we uphold the tenets of the Agile Manifesto by studying processes like Lean, Scrum, Systems Thinking, eXtreme Programming (XP), Organizational Effectiveness, and most importantly, practicing and giving back to the Agile community. Once you have decided to adopt the Agile methodology, we hope that you too will sign the Oath of Non-Allegiance.

vimeopro.com/leandog/oath

1 Alistair Cockburn, http://alistair.cockburn.us/Oath+of+Non-Allegiance 2 Kent Beck, et al http://www.agilemanifesto.org
3 Michele Sliger and Stacia Broderick. The Software Project Manager's Bridge to Agility, (Addison-Wesley: 2008)
4 Babatunde A. Ogunnaike and W. Harmon Ray. Process Dynamics, Modeling and Control. (NY: Oxford University, 1994)

Company Ecosystem

A company ecosystem represents a big-picture view of the whole organization's environment. Because an organization is composed of many interconnected parts, understanding the ecosystem can provide key insights into where bottlenecks may occur during software or business development. Most importantly, it can reveal areas that may help or hinder an Agile transformation.

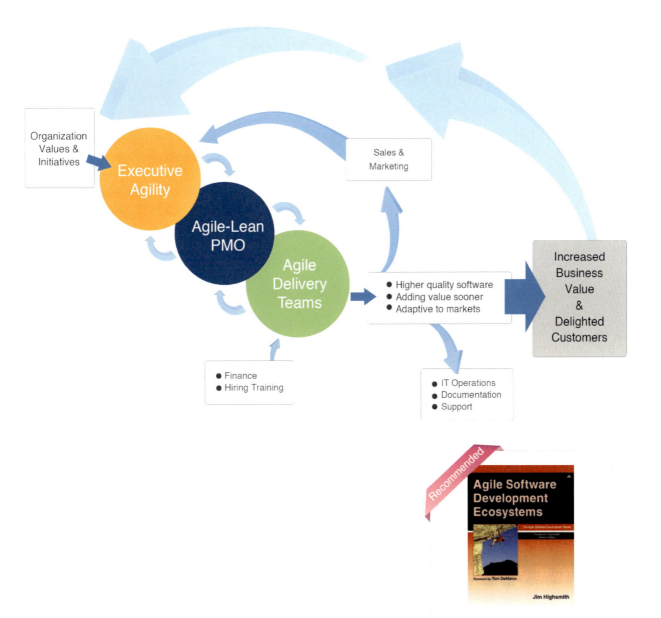

vimeopro.com/leandog/ecosystem

"Agile Software Development Ecosystems"
By Jim Highsmith

Agile Benefits Realized

A 2013 survey by VersionOne found that the top three reasons for adopting Agile were: to increase productivity, accelerate time to market, and more easily manage changing priorities. Beyond that, there are a number of other important aspects to a business that can be improved by adopting Agile.

Here are some of the significant benefits reported by organizations as a result of adopting Agile methodologies, according to the VersionOne study.

92% Managing **Changing Priorities**
87% Increased **Productivity**
86% Increase **Project Visibility**
86% Improve **Team Morale**
83% Accelerated **Time to Market**
82% Enhance **Software Quality**
82% Improve **IT & Business Objectives Alignment**
82% Reduce **Risk**
78% Simplify **Development Process**
74% Improve **Engineering Discipline**

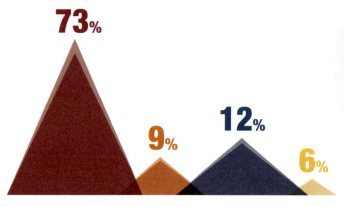

Getting projects completed is important to any business, 73% of respondents to the survey found that their projects were completed faster after adopting Agile.

VersionOne, "State of Agile Survey, 2013" Survey includes information for 7042 participants
http://www.versionone.com/pdf/2013-state-of-agile-survey.pdf

Chapter 2

Agile Concepts

In this chapter
- Agile Concepts
- Whole Team
- Open Workspace
- T-Shaped People
- Sustainable Pace
- Information Radiators
- Frequent Releases
- Story Card Wall
- Agile Triangle
- Cone of Uncertainty

Agile Concepts

Building software using Agile approaches is a "team sport". The concepts discussed are about the people; how we work and collaborate together. Enhancing communication and collaboration is a key theme of many of our concepts.

Essential

- Do we have everyone on the team that we need?
- Is our team located in the same space?
- Are people broadly skilled, knowledgeable, and able to help each other?
- Do we have the workload set so we don't need heroic efforts?
- Is it easy for the team and non-team members to understand where we stand?
- Do we have inexpensive and simple ways to communicate?

"The Agile Samurai: How Agile Masters Deliver Great Software"
By Jonathan Rasmusson

 vimeopro.com/leandog/agile-concepts

Whole Team

The Whole Team Approach states that everyone is accountable for the quality of the product. This approach brings the entire team together to work as a unit and share responsibility for producing high quality software. Whole Team is the glue of Agile practices; it holds all the other practices together.

Essential

- Whole team shares workspace
- Team members are 100% dedicated to the team's work, not allocated to other work outside the team
- Work comes to the team, the team doesn't form based on the funding of projects
- Avoid shared talent between teams. DBAs and other technical specialists are available on demand, but are preferably T-Shaped and on the team
- Poly-pairing encouraged
- Team is led, not managed
- Team communicates and collaborates continuously
- Team is accountable for results

Advanced

- Business partners are co-located with team
- Team is not named after the project or department, instead they have their own team identity (example: code monkeys, red fish blue fish).

Teams must be self-empowered; put the right people in the right seats.

Why Teams?

Organizational boundaries typically increase cost by over 25%, creating buffers that slow down response time and interfere with communication [1].

"The Art of Agile Development"
By James Shore
(Chapter 3)

 vimeopro.com/leandog/whole-team

1 Mary Poppendieck, Poppendieck LLC

Open Workspace

Face-to-face communication is extremely valuable. In an Open Workspace the team uses open seating to facilitate communication, and shorten feedback loops and ideation. It is the hardest practice to implement, but transparency and increased communication make it the most valuable.

Essential Guidelines

Workspace
- General rule is 150 square feet per team member: adequate space for moving, sitting, and collaborating
- There are no assigned seats
- Teams do not have other personal space (like cubes)
- Two small breakout rooms are available for meetings or privacy
- White boards, cork boards or flip charts provide a dynamic workspace as well as privacy for teams
- Team uses open seating to facilitate paired programming and communication
- Leadership sits with the team
- Have teams in a highly visible area, be proud to show the space to customers
- Team Members have a "locker room" to store personal belongings
- Furniture is movable without permission, team has ability to form the space
- Allow picture skins on laptops (family, dogs, sports, etc)
- Allow team to be creative and introduce fun into the workspace

Team
- Noise equals collaboration and communication, quiet is "bad" (Parent's Ear Rule: bad sounds are complete silence or kicking & screaming)
- "Hey Team" cooperation when roadblocks are discovered
- Teams sit facing each other, not with backs to each other
- Requires that facilities and leadership understand the goals, and is engaged with the team
- All rules deserve team discussion

Open Workspace

Equipment
- Tables have wheels or can easily be moved
- Power comes from floor or ceiling, not from cubicle walls that don't move
- Team room has one team phone, not one per person. Provide cell phones, phone booths, Skype ID's, etc. to co-workers
- Easy or permanent access to video conference equipment to connect with customers and other teams. Face-to-face communication is valued highly
- Headphones available for Skype calls, remote pairing
- Wireless networks improve flexibility

Advanced Guidelines

Workspace
- Provide white noise generators
- Food station with coffee nearby, but not on center island
- Rolling tool box for office supplies, clearly labeled and replenished
- Teams should have access to bright desirable spaces and not be relegated to closed conference rooms and basements
- One large breakout room available for meetings or privacy
- Windows are tools, the team is allowed to have things taped to them and use dry eraser markers on them
- Two phone booths available for personal conversations

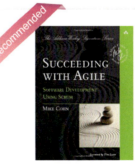

"Succeeding with Agile: Software Development Using Scrum"
By Mike Cohn

Open Workspace

Advanced (continued)

Team (Working Agreements)
- Pick one day a week, perhaps after the Friday daily Stand Up, to clean the work area for 15 minutes; ensure that visible info is necessary (look for stale information)
- Music is OK, team agrees on rules around this
- If something isn't working for facilities management, voice concerns at the retrospective meeting
- If something isn't working for the team, it will go on the roadblock wall
- All rules should be prominent in team space (e.g.: leave three feet around perimeter for fire safety, no cords that people can trip on, etc)

Equipment
- Projector(s) or TVs readily available, set up, and ready to use
- Magnetic whiteboards allow teams to slide cards around easily
- Each conference room has a high-quality speaker phone/video conference phone
- Large monitors set up to connect laptops, have two side-by-side
- Toys should be prevalent: fun fosters innovation
- Team members choose type of laptop (Apple or PC) – OK to have both kinds on the team if the team agrees
- Everyone has laptops to improve mobility, encouraged to take home and study craft
- Team has easy access to a plotter to print information radiators or TVs to radiate information digitally
- Printer is capable of printing on index cards
- Have hand sanitizer readily available to prevent spreading germs

 vimeopro.com/leandog/open-space

T-Shaped People

A T-Shaped person is an individual who has deep knowledge of a specialized skill set but also has acquired tangential, related skills. T-Shaped people are also interested in continuously broadening their knowledge as well as deepening a core skill set. T-Shaped people are also known as generalizing-specialists or "Renaissance Man" workers.

Essential

- People are encouraged to learn and pair in all roles
- Collaboration between team members to build T-Shaped People
- Team members cross-train each other in technical and domain specialized knowledge
- Team creates an environment that facilitates and encourages continual learning
- Activities such as pairing, job shadowing, lunch-n-learns, book clubs, and open discussions are used frequently

Advanced

- Anyone on the team can pick up any story card
- Team members are encouraged to pick story cards in areas with which they are unfamiliar as a learning challenge
- Team will focus learning activities around bottlenecks
- Create cross-team communities of practice around technical specialties, domain knowledge areas, or any other area of interest

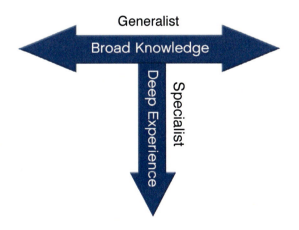

 vimeopro.com/leandog/tshaped-people

"Management 3.0: Leading Agile Developers, Developing Agile Leaders"
By Jurgen Appelo
(Chapter 13)

Sustainable Pace

A Sustainable Pace is a constant pace that a development team should be able to maintain indefinitely, to ensure the team has time to plan, think, rest, and deliver effectively.

Essential

- Team members typically works a 40-hour week
- Includes daily work responsibilities, training opportunities and sustainable fun
- Must give enough time to include all regular team activities such as initiation, planning, development, testing, and deployment
- Avoid the death march or the need for heroic efforts; instead, focus on repetitive delivery of high-quality software

Advanced

- Team pace should include enough slack, mental downtime, or development time to allow for other activities which foster creativity and innovation
- Team is evaluated on performance, not presence (Result-Only Focus)
- All regular work week constraints are removed from the core team (i.e. All team members are required to be at their desks for work day by 8 a.m.)

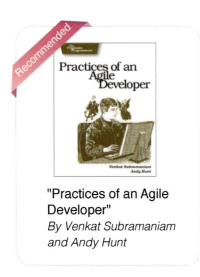

"Practices of an Agile Developer"
By Venkat Subramaniam and Andy Hunt

 vimeopro.com/leandog/sustainable-pace

Information Radiators

Information Radiators display important project information simply, communicating information even from across the room. Use Information Radiators to map project statuses so the team knows the status at all times: what's coded, what's verified and what's to come.

Essential

- Anyone should be able to review the information displayed and easily understand it
- Key charts include:
  - Release Plan & Roadblocks
  - Product Value Map
  - Burn Up & Velocity
  - Story Card Wall
  - Unit Test & Acceptance Test Coverage
- Used for continuous communication and information radiation
- Presented in a casual way (no complexity, just charts on walls)
- Team Blocks & Escalation

Advanced

- Team decides what is visible
- Flow of information is centered around the workspace. The walls should tell a story to the team and customer
- Charts track everything from future project requests to fully-tested stories
- Other helpful items to be considered:
  - Organizational Value map
  - Program Demand Management
  - Persona Map
  - Ideation Wall (to capture and compare new ideas or potential work)

vimeopro.com/leandog/radiators

27

Information Radiators

Clear communication requires a validation of shared understanding. Diagrams, flowcharts, and other visual aids are an excellent way to ensure that ideas discussed are actually understood in the intended manner.

Clear Communication

1. Clear communication is the foundation

"I'm glad we all agree"

2. Get those mental models out on the table

"Ah!"

3. An explicit model allows convergence through iteration

"Ah!"

4. A genuinely shared understanding

"I'm glad we're all agreed then"

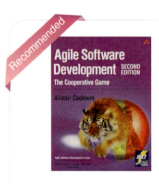

"Agile Software Development: The Cooperative Game"
By Alistair Cockburn

Information Radiators
Invented around the year 2000
By Alistair Cockburn

Frequent Releases

Frequent Releases are intended to shorten feedback cycles and improve responsiveness by deploying code in short cycles. This improves productivity by providing more opportunities to handle new or changing requirements, or adjusting priorities of planned work in response to business or user needs.

Essential

- At the end of each iteration the software should be ready for production, the business determines if it is released
- Apply fixed capacity against a fixed date, prioritizing cards by business value. The capacity and schedule are fixed, but the scope is flexible
- Fixed capacity and fixed scope allow for flexible dates
- The team (including the product owner) must agree on what a completed state means for individual features and releases

Advanced

- Working software is frequently delivered to business partners in small, functional chunks
- Releases are scheduled based on the input and needs of business partners
- Teams strive to reduce the risk of large, "big bang" releases by reducing the size of each release, and automating the release process to improve repeatability and minimize the cost of releasing frequently.
- Create a release schedule to help shape the direction of the product or initiative

"The Art of Agile Development"
by James Shore (Chapter 8)

"Practices of an Agile Developer"
By Venkat Subramaniam and Andy Hunt (Chapter 4)

 vimeopro.com/leandog/frequent-releases

Story Card Wall

The Story Card Wall is an information radiator tool used in the team's workspace. It is an effective way to display the status of each card in its current iteration. The story card wall is broken up into columns reflecting each function necessary to the process. Story cards can be index cards or Post-its®.

Essential

- Must be on a physical wall in the team's space
- Positioned in a clean, well-lit place
- All team members move cards
- Cards should be written, not printed (easy to change vs. edit tool/reprint)
- The definition of 'complete' should be clear
- Personal WIP limits: no more than one card per person can be in play at a time
- Everyone on the team can read and explain the story card wall
- Use color coding to differentiate cards of different work types - legend Minimal Marketable Feature Sets (MMF)

"User Stories Applied: For Agile Software Development"
By Mike Cohn

 vimeopro.com/leandog/story-card-wall

Story Card Wall

Advanced

- Portable magnetic dry erase card walls are the best
- Enough room around wall for team to gather
- Pictures on magnets show card owner
- Retrospective items on wall are not necessarily part of a Story Card Wall. However, some teams do maintain an area to list topics that team members want to discuss at an upcoming retrospective.
- Stand up should be in front of wall
- Visual sign explain specific transition criteria for cards to move between statuses on the board (e.g. what has to be done/verified for each card in "Development" before it can move to "Testing")
- Anything in progress has a name attached to it
- Cards are easy to read from a distance
- Team establishes an overall team WIP limit (in addition to personal WIP limits) to reflect team's sustainable capacity
- Team writes "Created", "Started", and "Completed/Accepted" dates on cards to facilitate tracking of lead time / cycle time
- On-Hold Metrics: Some teams keep track of "Hold" time - i.e. when a card cannot be worked on continuously once it has been started. Cards are annotated with hash marks to represent any full- or half-day increments during which the card had to be placed "On Hold" for some reason. (Some overlap with Roadblocks, but sometimes reveals/highlights different process problems)

Agile Triangle

Agile teams are often asked to be "adaptive, flexible, or agile," but also asked to stick with a plan. A traditional plan is based on scope, schedule and cost. An agile triangle turns the triangle upside down and has very different goals of customer delight, building quality products while speeding up the development process. The Agile Triangle in simpler words changes the way we view success [1].

Essential

Question should be: "Can we release this product now?"
- Look at the value of a functionality over implementing all the requirements
- Quality today - current iteration or release of product
- Quality tomorrow - release that continues to respond to business changes both anticipated and un-anticipated
- Constraints - scope, schedule, cost - not unimportant, but not the goal of the project

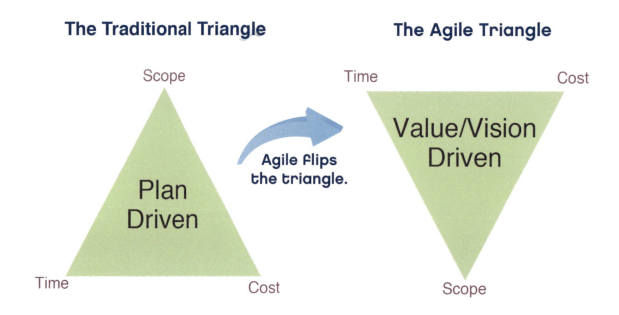

[1] "Agile Project Management: Creating Innovative Product" by Jim Highsmith

Cone of Uncertainty

The Cone of Uncertainty describes the amount of uncertainty during different time periods of a project. At the beginning of a project, it's hard to estimate activity with a high level of accuracy and confidence because little is known about the product or the results. As you begin researching and developing the product, the uncertainty level will decrease.

Essential

- Estimates at beginning of project are very vague
- Estimates and project plans need to be re-estimated on a regular basis
- Uncertainties should be built into the estimates
- Uncertainties should be visible in project plans

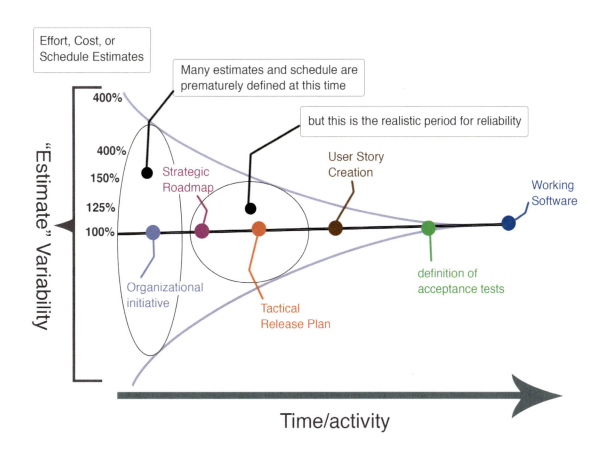

Chapter 3

Agile Process

In this chapter
- Agile Process
- Kanban
- Scrum Framework
- Story Card Writing
- Estimation & Sizing
- Sprints/Iterations
- Customer Collaboration

Agile Process

There are several popular models: eXtreme Programming (XP), Scrum, Crystal, Kanban, and others. All have a common solution for improving the outcomes of software development through concepts like "the minimum responsible amount" of many artifacts. Consider specific circumstances to figure out what might be the best fit for each situation. The LeanDog Agile Discussion Guide gives you an idea of the many tools and approaches that are available for addressing specific challenges that your team may encounter.

Essential

- Recognize that current processes, organizational structures, culture and approaches are usually the key causes of throughput/quality problems - not your people
- Coach your people on finding problems and challenges: finding, identifying and talking about problems is EXPECTED
- Based on the problems and challenges that are being highlighted, we can pick processes and approaches to help resolve them

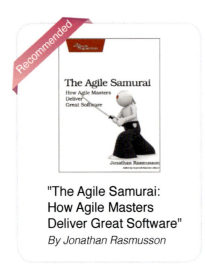

"The Agile Samurai: How Agile Masters Deliver Great Software"
By Jonathan Rasmusson

 vimeopro.com/leandog/agile-process

Kanban

In the 1950's, Taiichi Ohno began using Kanban in Toyota's primary machine shop. Translating to "signboard" or "billboard", Kanban is a visual scheduling system that helps a team determine what to produce, when to produce it, and how much to produce.

Essential

- Visualize workflow and picture the product in each state—from concept to deployment
- Limit work in progress (WIP) to prevent your team from becoming overwhelmed, and keep progress continuous and steady.
- Manage flow in order to allow and prepare for changes that will occur within the iteration
- Make team, queue and practice policies explicit so your team knows how to participate properly, ensuring a smoother iteration
- When a TEMPORARY surplus in capacity occurs, give precedence to helping other team members complete any work already in progress, before taking on new tasks/cards

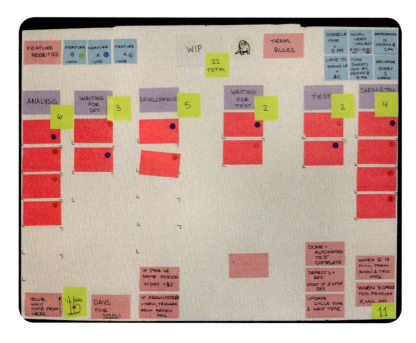

"Kanban: Successful Evolutionary Change for your Technology Business"
By David J Anderson

 vimeopro.com/leandog/kanban

Kanban

Advanced

- Implement feedback mechanisms like operations review, mentorship and daily production meetings to ensure demands are being met while identifying where improvements can be made
- Improve collaboratively with a scientific approach: continuous reflective analysis paired with small adjustments, encouraging timely evolution at a sustainable pace
- Periodically review/revisit team WIP limits with team, customers and stakeholders, especially when changes to team's composition occur
- WIP limits are intended to facilitate the flow of work through the team by making it easy to decide whether or not the team is ready to take on new work. As such, WIP limits should never be used as a negotiation tool - only as a collaboration tool

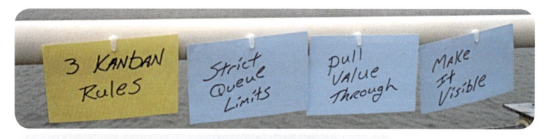

$$\text{Delivery Rate} = \frac{\text{Cycle Time}}{\text{Lead Time}} \quad \text{Work in Progress}$$

Decrease WIP in order to decrease cycle time (delivery rate).
Smaller stories in process will come out faster.

Scrum Framework

Scrum is an Agile development model that consists of small teams working interdependently. The teams work together, but focus on their own tasks and must be capable of self management and decision-making. Scrum is based around a "sprint," which is generally a 1-4 week period for delivering a working part of the system. At the end of a sprint the results are delivered, then reviewed, and the next sprint is started [1].

Essential

- A product backlog is created and prioritized by the product owner
- The product owner selects story cards from the product backlog and adds them to the sprint backlog, deciding what cards get implemented
- A sprint (or iteration) is a short amount of time to get a significant amount of work done. Team selects the duration, LeanDog recommends 1-2 weeks
- The team meets each day to assess their progress; a "daily scrum"
- The Scrum Master keeps the team focused on their goals
- At the end of each sprint, the work that was selected from the product backlog should be released to the customer, put on a store shelf, or shown to a stakeholder
- Every sprint ends with a sprint review and retrospective
- When a new sprint begins, the team selects another group of story cards from the product backlog
- The cycle repeats until there are no more story cards to be played in the product backlog, budget is unavailable, or the deadline has passed. Using the scrum process ensures that the most valuable parts of the product are built first

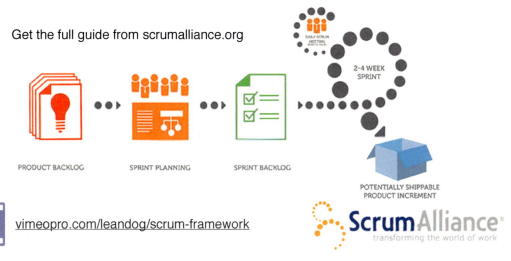

Get the full guide from scrumalliance.org

vimeopro.com/leandog/scrum-framework

[1] Scrum Alliance, http://www.scrumalliance.org/pages/what_is_scrum
Picture source: Scrum Alliance, http://www.scrumalliance.org/pages/what_is_scrum

Scrum Framework

the Scrum Process Framework

The Scrum process framework was originally named and described by Ken Schwaber, Jeff Sutherland, and Mike Beedle in the mid 1990s. It takes its name from the comparison to Rugby made in the 1986 HBR article: "The New New Product Development Game". In 2001 the term "agile" was coined to describe processes that focused on collaborative iterative and incremental development approaches. Originally Scrum was one of the named processes that called themselves "agile" including processes such as Extreme Programming, Feature Driven Development, Crystal, and others. Today Scrum is the dominant process framework in part because of its simplicity.

Scrum is intentionally incomplete. It's a framework that relies on inspection and adaptation to improve and add to the basic process framework.

Roles

The Scrum Framework uses three "super roles" that satisfy the basic concerns of software development.

- The **Product Owner** is responsible for building the right product.
- The **Team** is responsible for building the product right.
- The **Scrum Master** is responsible for keeping the process healthy so people can perform at their best

Traditional software development roles are often mapped to one or more of these super roles.

Artifacts

The basic artifacts in Scrum are there to aid with visibility and transparency.

- The **Product Backlog** makes the product features and plan visible.
- The **Sprint Backlog** makes the team's delivery plan visible.
- **Burndown Charts** show the pace of work in progress, what's accomplished, and what's remaining.

Ceremonies

Scrum ceremonies are working meetings where the team plans, inspects, and adapts.

- ◇ **Sprint Planning** is where the team creates their delivery plan for highest priority product backlog items and commits to the amount of work they believe they can complete during a fixed-length Sprint.
- ◇ The **Daily Scrum** is for the team to reflect on where they are so far with their sprint commitment and plan their day's work.
- ◇ The **Sprint Review and Retrospective** is where the team inspects the product they've produced, the performance relative to their plan, and adapts their process, product, and plan in response.

Values & Principles

All agile processes, and most effective processes, emphasize core values and principles that guide process tailoring and adaptation. Below is a distillation of core Scrum principles. Use these principles to assess process health and guide routine process improvement.

Transparency & Visibility

We're open and transparent about the way we make decisions and work. We keep the basis for our decisions, our work, and our progress visible.

Feedback: Inspect & Adapt

We continuously assess the quality of the product we're building, the quality of our plan, and the effectiveness of our process. Then, using that understanding, adapt or make changes to the product design, the plan, or the process.

Responsibility: Individual and Team

We take responsibility as a team. We **self-organize** in a way that helps us keep our commitments. We understand that we collectively share goals. In a healthy Scrum team, you'd never hear the phrase:

"It's not my problem, the hole's in their side of the boat."

I, as an individual, take responsibility for my commitments to the team. I do so by understanding my role, and my work and then take action to keep my commitments. I actively take responsibility for building the skills I need to help me succeed.

The Team

The team is composed of all the roles and skills necessary to build, test, and document software of sufficient quality that it could be released. The team usually includes:
- developers
- architects
- testers
- business analysts
- UI designers
- technical writers

Product Owner

A successful product must be **valuable** to the business **usable** to users, and **feasible** to build. While a single person may fill the product owner role, it's common for a cross functional team to hold product ownership responsibility.

The product owner is responsible for creating and maintaining a **Prioritized Product Backlog**

Product Backlog

The team works together in the Sprint Planning Meeting to create a **Sprint Backlog** that contains the work tasks they'll need deliver working software.

Daily Scrum

Reflect on what was done the prior day
Plan what to do today
Raise issues stopping progress

Day — The smallest cycle of work – you can't extend this one if you don't finish what you planned

Scrum Master

The Scrum Master focuses on making sure the process is working, that everyone understands and fills their role, that collaboration is effective, that visibility is kept high, and that the team keeps focus on the goals of the current sprint and product release.

The Scrum Master is a process facilitator, NOT process policeman.

The Scrum Master keeps a watchful eye on everything, coaching, facilitating, and **removing impediments** that block progress

Sprint

A fixed time-box for delivering software usually 1-4 weeks

Sprint Planning

The product owner shows up "ready" with details for high priority backlog items. The team builds their plan and commits.

Sprint Backlog

The delivery tasks that turn backlog items into working software

Sprint Burndown

Makes progress visible during this sprint. Are we making progress? Where is work getting bottlenecked?

Release Burndown

Makes progress visible for the the upcoming release. Will we make our date? Or, are we fooling ourselves?

Potentially Shippable Software Increment

It may take more software to be valuable to users, but it had better not require more testing and bug fixing

Sprint Review & Retrospective

Demonstrate and critique the working **Product**
Discuss the **Progress** relative to the plan
Reflect on the way you've been working (your **Process**) and change it as necessary

Repeat

Repeat as necessary – probably forever

Illustration by Jeff Patton

Story Card Writing

A Story Card is the unit of each deliverable for an Agile team. Story Cards include a sentence or two describing a needed function. Rather than representing detailed requirements, story cards are a "placeholder for a conversation". Story cards are testable and include acceptance criteria. The details are elaborated upon via conversation between the customer, and the delivery team.

Essential

- Cards are handwritten
- Cards should follow the format: "In order to (X), As a (Y), I want (Z);" these are the Values, Roles, and Goals of the card requested feature
- Spike cards exist (see Spike practice for definition)
- Follow INVEST rule (see next page)
- Story cards should represent a vertical slice of the application and deliver business value
- Story cards are sized to fit an iteration
- Use the 3 C's: the Card, the Conversation AND the Confirmation
- The definition of "done" must be clear

Advanced

- Developer pairs with BA/product owner to write cards
- Utilize Story Mapping (see page 90) as a tool to identify stories and priorities

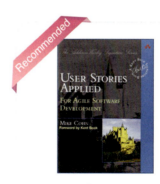

"User Stories Applied: For Agile Software Development"
By Mike Cohn

Story Card Writing

Invest Rule

- **Independent**
  Story Cards should be independent of each other

- **Negotiable**
  The card should be a short description of the deliverable without too many details. The details should be worked out during the "conversation" phase

- **Valuable**
  Each story must be of value to the customer and have a value given to it

- **Estimable**
  In order to plan and prioritize, developers need to be able to ballpark or estimate the effort to complete the story

- **Small**
  Ideally the story should be small typically taking no more than 2-3 days

- **Testable**
  If you cannot test it then you will never know when you are done, so a story needs to be testable for confirmation to take place

Values, Roles, & Goals

Business Value: In order to _____

User Role/Persona: As a _____

Goals/Perform Something: I want to _____

Or, Alternate Format:

As a __(who)__

I Want __(what)__

So that __(why)__

The 3 C's

User stories have three critical aspects:

- **Card**
  Stories are written on cards. Each card does not contain all of the information, but just enough to show the requirements of the feature. Cards are used during planning.

- **Conversation**
  The requirements on each card are communicated from the customer to the delivery team members through conversation: exchange of thoughts, opinions, and feelings. These conversations happen many times before/during release planning, during iteration planning, and again when the story is ready for implementation.

- **Confirmation**
  After running acceptance tests and confirming with the customer that the tests were successful, a card has been completed.

Estimation & Sizing

Estimating and Sizing are techniques for evaluating the size / complexity of delivering features in order to facilitate planning and guide investment decisions. A good planning process based on a reliable estimation and sizing approach reduces risk and uncertainty, supports better decision making, establishes trust and conveys information.

Essential
- Use relative sizes
- Planning Poker - Story Points, T-shirt sizes, etc.
- Team understands it's not just time, it's complexity
- Very few large cards
- Cards which the team feels are too large/complex to complete within an iteration should be broken down into smaller / less complex cards
- Re-estimate when significant new information is uncovered, as it changes complexity
- Management understands differences of size/estimating vs. hours
- Re-estimate in the event of team changes
- Make all cards as small as possible
- Consider all cards small "By Definition"
- Rewrite / breakdown / decompose card when a smaller slice is found.

Advanced
- Measure and account for "Card Growth" between planning and delivery (e.g. 1 card in the backlog may turn into, on average, 1.25 cards delivered, due to some fraction of the cards being able to be decomposed into smaller slices when we discuss them in detail with the product owner)

"Agile Estimating & Planning"
By Mike Cohn

 vimeopro.com/leandog/estimation

Sprints/Iterations

A Sprint/Iteration is a set period of time for measuring a development team's throughput. Sprints/Iterations are one to two weeks in length with shorter iterations being the goal.

Essential

- Work is organized to be completed in short time frames (1 - 2 weeks)
- Story cards worked on during an iteration must meet the team's definition of done and get Product Owner acceptance to be considered complete
- Team gets credit for functional, tested and approved code

Advanced

- Unplanned work is noted at retrospectives

Sprint/Iteration Process Flow

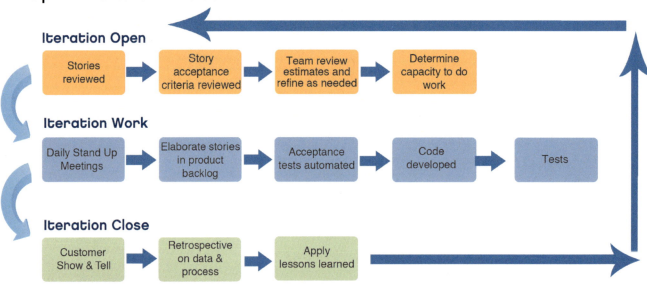

 vimeopro.com/leandog/sprints-iterations

Customer Collaboration

Customer Collaboration is the practice of including your customer throughout development. Only the customer can tell you what they want, and collaboration allows you to listen to their needs instead of guessing at what they need. The customer drives the requirements, prioritization, and review of work. While it is not always possible to have customers on site, you must make interaction with them a priority.

Essential

- Customer must be clearly identified, and roles and responsibilities clearly defined
- Customer may take the form of customer proxy, product owner, business stakeholder, end-user or any combination of these roles. Customer owns the responsibility of driving work in the team that meets overall product goals and objectives for software being built and delivered by focusing the team's efforts on the highest priorities, highest business value features, and stories for release
- Customer works closely with team to break features down to stories
- Customer determines minimal marketable features and signs off on completed stories supporting those features for release
- Grooming of product backlog is a collaborative effort between customer and team to adapt to changing product goals and objectives
- Customer listens to the team, the team listens to the customer
- The definition of "done" must be clear

Advanced

- Create personas as a tool to better understand customers and their expectations
- Co-locate with the team to increase collaboration and communication
- Attend all team meetings (stand-ups, retrospectives, sprint planning)

 vimeopro.com/leandog/customer-collaboration

"Collaboration: How Leaders Avoid the Traps, Create Unity, and Reap Big Results"
By Morten Hansen

Chapter 4

Leadership

In this chapter
- Leadership Role
- Servant Leadership
- Six Thinking Hats
- Collaboration 8
- Fist to 5

Leadership Role

In order to support the successful adaptation of Agile and uphold its values, principles and practices, an organization's leadership needs to create a culture of continuous improvement. This section covers servant leadership, an important leadership style along with other collaboration techniques that allow teams to self organize and make decisions. It is important that the entire organization, from the top down, understands the notion of servant leadership and agrees on a team-based decision-making process.

Essential

- Practice servant leadership
- Establish team based decision processes
- Enjoy seeing team learn
- Remove roadblocks

Advanced

- Leads by example by practicing Agile practices such as:
    - Daily Stand-ups
    - Information Radiators
    - Retrospectives
    - Making work visible
    - Limiting work in progress
    - Open workspace

Servant Leadership

A servant leader is an individual who puts others first. They are good communicators, collaborators, systematic thinkers, and lead with moral authority. A leader with moral authority is one who is worthy of respect, inspires trust and confidence, and establishes a quality standard for performance. They accept and delegate responsibility, share power and control, and create a culture of accountability.

Essential

Seven Pillars of Servant Leadership

- Person of character - maintain integrity, demonstrate humility and serve a higher purpose
- Puts people first - displays a servant's heart, is mentor-minded, and shows care and concern
- Skilled communicator - demonstrates empathy, invites feedback, communicates persuasively
- Compassionate collaborator - expresses appreciation, builds teams, and negotiates conflict
- Foresight - visionary, displays creativity, and exercises sound judgement
- System thinker - comfortable with complexity, demonstrates adaptability, and considers the "Greater Good"
- Leads with moral authority - granted by others

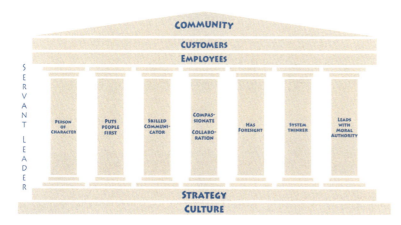

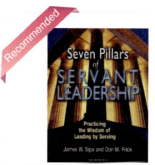

"Seven Pillars of Servant Leadership: Practicing the Wisdom of Leading by Serving" *By James W. Sipe & Don M. Frick*

 vimeopro.com/leandog/servant-leadership

Page source: "Seven Pillars of Servant Leadership: Practicing the Wisdom of Leading by Serving" by James W. Sipe & Don M. Frick

Six Thinking Hats

Four people try to describe a house: one stands in front, one in back, one on each side. They can't agree on the correct view. We've all been in that situation. The Six Thinking Hats® creates an environment that encourages "parallel thinking" (versus argument) where everyone in the discussion looks in the same direction at the same time.

Essential

Six Thinking Hats:
- **White Hat:** calls for information known or needed. "The facts, just the facts."
- **Yellow Hat:** symbolizes optimism. Under this hat you explore the positives and probe for value and benefit.
- **Black Hat:** is judgment - the devil's advocate, or why something may not work. Spot the difficulties and dangers; where things might go wrong. Probably the most powerful and useful of the hats, but a problem if overused
- **Red Hat:** Signifies feelings, and intuition. When using this hat you can express emotions and feelings, and share fears, likes, dislikes, loves, and hates.
- **Green Hat:** focuses on creativity: the possibilities, alternatives, and new ideas. It's an opportunity to express new concepts and new perceptions.
- **Blue Hat:** is used to manage the thinking process. It's the control mechanism that ensures the Six Thinking Hats® guidelines are observed
- The four major benefits of Six Thinking Hats®
    - Power – the group is looking and working in the same direction
    - Time saving – thinking in parallel prevents argument and saves time
    - Removal of ego – minimizes emotion, creates focus
    - One thing at a time – minimizes confusion created by argument

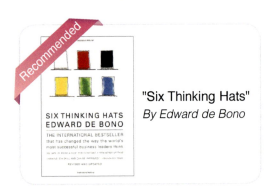

"Six Thinking Hats"
By Edward de Bono

vimeopro.com/leandog/6-thinking-hats

Page source: "Six Thinking Hats" by Edward De Bono

Six Thinking Hats

Download Our App

LeanDog Agile Tools

6 Thinking Hats

LeanDog

Rules of the Game:

- Each hat represents a state of mind. For example, when the group "wears" the white hat, the only acceptable contributions to the discussion involve facts—nothing else.
- While there is no order to follow, you should always begin and end with the "Blue Hat".

© Edward de Bono, *Six Thinking Hats*

Blue

Facilitator always the first and last step. Calm, oversees dialogue and moves the discussion along.

Black

The Devil's advocate, focus on potential pitfalls or problems.

Yellow

Assess all of the positive aspects of the problem or situation.

Green

Formulate a new idea based on the new data collected from the other hats.

Red

Explore emotions and feelings, without the need to justify or explain why.

White

Objective and logical, concerned only with facts and figures.

Collaboration 8

Collaboration 8 is a slight twist on Jurgen Appelo's "7 Levels of Authority". We use it as a fast and simple means of identifying who should be involved in the decisions, creating operating agreements and making personnel involvement publicly visible. The Joker card is a LeanDog addition. This card is played when someone sets expectations one way, but does not continue to play by that agreement.

Essential

Here is our adaptation, which might be better described as the levels of collaboration: "The 7 Levels of Authority" (plus the Joker)

- **Tell:** I know exactly what I want and we need to do it this way
- **Sell:** I consider this to be my responsibility, but I will get buy-in from others
- **Consult:** I want your insight but I will decide how we do the work
- **Agree:** I want to work together
- **Advise:** I want to give you insight and let you do the work
- **Inquire:** I trust you to do the work but I want to understand so I can support you
- **Delegate:** I will support whatever decision you make
- **Joker:** You are violating the agreement that we have made earlier

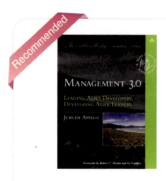

"Management 3.0 Leading Agile Developers, Agile Leaders" *By Jurgen Appelo*

 vimeopro.com/leandog/collaboration-8

Page source: Michael "Doc" Norton's blog: http://www.docondev.com/2012/04/collaboration-8.html
Page source: Jurgen Appelo Delegation 7 content: http://www.management30.com/delegation-poker/

Collaboration 8

Download Our App

LeanDog Agile Tools

Rules of the Game:
Collaboration 8 cards are an Agile tool for estimating individual commitments to projects without the influence of other team members.
- Each member of the discussion shows their card at the same time
- The card they show reflects the level of their commitment to the topic at hand.

© Tannenbaum, R. and Schmidt, W. How to Choose a Leadership Pattern
Jurgen Appelo. Management 3.0. Delegation 7 cards

1 Tell

I know exactly what I want and we need to do it this way

2 Sell

I consider this to be my responsibility, but I will get buy-in from others

3 Consult

I want your insight but I will decide how we do the work

4 Agree

I want to work together.

5 Advise

I want to give you insight and let you do the work

6 Inquire

I trust you to do the work but I want to understand so I can support you

7 Delegate

I will support whatever decision you make

J Joker

You are violating the agreement that we have made earlier.

Fist to 5

The Fist to Five approach combines the speed of thumbs up/down with the degrees of agreement. Using this approach, people vote using their hands and fingers to represent their degree of support.

Essential

- Fist - A "no" vote, a way to block consensus. "I need to talk more on the proposal and require changes for it to pass."
- 1 Finger - "I need to discuss certain issues and have some suggestions."
- 2 Fingers - "I am more comfortable with the proposal but would like to discuss some minor issues."
- 3 Fingers - "I'm not in total agreement, but feel comfortable to let this decision or proposal pass without further discussion."
- 4 Fingers - "I think it's a good idea/decision and will work for it."
- 5 Fingers - "It's a great idea and I will be one of the leaders implementing it."
- If anyone holds up fewer than three fingers, they should be given the opportunity to share their concerns with the team.
- Teams continue the Fist-to-Five process until they achieve consensus (a minimum of three fingers or higher) or determine they must move on to the next issue.
- There must be a reasonable level of trust and cooperation amongst the group
- Ensure that everyone understands the voting system.

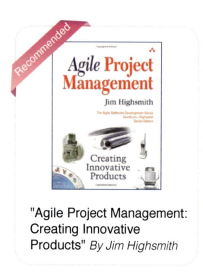

"Agile Project Management: Creating Innovative Products" *By Jim Highsmith*

vimeopro.com/leandog/fist-to-5

Page source: Fletcher, A. (2002). FireStarter Youth Power Curriculum: Participant Guidebook. Olympia, WA: Freechild Project.

Chapter 5

Scrum Master / Iteration Manager

In this chapter
- Scrum Master / Iteration Manager
- Daily Scrum/Stand Up
- Sprint / Iteration Planning
- Show & Tell
- Retrospectives
- Velocity
- Roadblocks

Scrum Master / Iteration Manager

This person is the servant leader of the team sometimes known as Scrum Master or Iteration Manager. A key part of their role is helping the team adhere to the Agile values and principles. Once the team has agreed to certain approaches to their work, it's up to the Iteration Manager to remind the team of those commitments.

Essential

- Remove barriers between the development and the product owner, ensuring the development is directly driven by the product owner.
- Assist the product owner how to maximize return on investment (ROI), and meet their objectives through Agile approaches
- Improve the lives and productivity of the development team by facilitating creativity and empowerment
- Team champion of the process
- Influences practices and Agile values and principles without command and control activity
- Internal team coach and protector of the team
- Does not promise or schedule work on behalf of the team
- Keep information about the team's progress up to date and visible to all parties
- Identify, raise up and remove roadblocks

"The Agile Samurai: How Agile Masters Deliver Great Software"
By Jonathan Rasmusson

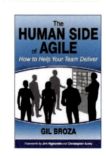

"The Human Side of Agile"
By Gil Broza

 vimeopro.com/leandog/iteration-manager

Agile Project Management with Scrum, Ken Schwaber

Daily Scrum/Stand Up

The Daily Stand Up is an Agile ceremony where the team meets for no more than 15 minutes every morning. Each person on the team reports briefly on what they did yesterday, what they are going to do today, and any concerns or roadblocks they are facing. Daily Stand Ups reduce the need for team meetings. They encourage accountability, as team members are aware of all work going on. Stand Ups also allow for mid-course corrections, encourage the team to solve problems on their own and help to notify managers early if there are any roadblocks.

Essential

- Collaborative activity with core team to share what they're working on and any roadblocks that are preventing forward progress on a story
- Occur daily at the same time for 15 minutes or less
- Address what was done yesterday / what will be done today / roadblocks
- Everybody attends and shows up on time
- Includes the customer so they can be informed and make adjustments
- There is no Stand Up leader - team facilitates

Advanced

- No stale roadblocks exist
- Debts help reinforce values at Stand Up (i.e.: late to Stand Up / playing with toys / pass to someone who went)
- Happens daily, regardless of priorities
- Sound signal to start Stand Up (Alarm / cow bell / gong)
- Team selects Stand Up time
- Team member records the roadblocks on the whiteboard so they are visible and cannot be ignored
- Team members are allowed to "Pass" if they have no new information to share and no roadblocks

 vimeopro.com/leandog/standup

Pictures source: Xavier Quesada Allue. Visual management. [Online] http://www.xqa.com.ar/visualmanagement/2009/04/daily-scrum-against-the-board/, 4/19/09.

Sprint/Iteration Planning

The Sprint/Iteration Planning meeting is held at the beginning of each new iteration to break down each of the features scheduled into individual stories. At the start of a new iteration, available work hours and projected velocity are set, the team reviews any card not completed in the prior iteration, business intent for new cards is established, the team re-estimates cards if necessary and the team determines what cards fit the new iteration and assigns them.

Essential

- Product Owner pulls stories from the product backlog to be played during the iteration
- Meeting includes the Iteration Close
    - Review of work completed during iteration, including roadblocks
    - Review of cards not completed during iteration
    - Velocity
- Meeting includes the Iteration Open
    - New story cards are reviewed for business intent/completeness
    - Team signs up for available work hours
    - Target velocity is established
- Business partners understand velocity and work within the budget to select stories that will be played in the new iteration

"Succeeding with Agile: Software Development Using Scrum"
By Mike Cohn

"Over-emphasis on velocity causes problems because of its wide [use] as a productivity measure[ment]. The proper use of velocity is as a calibration tool, a way to help do capacity-based planning, as Kent Beck describes in Extreme Programming: Embrace Change." [1]

"The ultimate expression of agility from a software perspective is continuous delivery and deployment. Our goal should not be productivity, but to design and deploy a great customer experience quickly—again and again over time." [1]

 vimeopro.com/leandog/sprint-iteration-planning

1 Jim Highsmith, http://jimhighsmith.com/2011/11/02/velocity-is-killing-agility/
Picture Source: http://d2lkacpp4m5oo7.cloudfront.net/wp-content/uploads/2010/05/AH-sprint-planning-meeting2.JPG

Show & Tell

Show and Tell is a demonstration of features completed during a sprint/iteration. This provides a forum for team members, customers and other stakeholders to review progress, provide feedback on new features and prioritize any changes needed to the delivered features. By using Show and Tell, teams maintain accountability to the customer.

Essential

- Core team, business owner and supporting roles demonstrate working code and acceptance tests completed during the iteration
- Customers attend
- Customer approves that the implementation met expectations
- Whole team attends
- Customer prioritizes changes immediately

 vimeopro.com/leandog/show-and-tell

"The Art of Agile Development"
By James Shore

Retrospectives

Retrospectives are meetings that take place after each iteration and are designed to help the team find ways to improve their processes and output. This meeting should be a safe environment in which to talk about what worked and what didn't work. The team votes on whether the items discussed during the retrospective should become cards to be played in the coming iteration.

Essential

- Core team applies continuous improvement principles to team activities; team discusses what went well and what didn't go well during the iteration to determine what needs to be improved
- Goal is to stress continuous improvement. Experimental changes, even those that fail, are encouraged
- All team members attend retro and assess how things went during the previous iteration
- Format includes a version of "what worked" and "what didn't work"
- Team decides which items to focus on; output lists actions
- Progress on action items is tracked and published
- Conducted after every iteration

Advanced

- Use safety checks to indicate that team members feel safe to bring up difficult topics
- Team holds spontaneous retrospectives for significant issues
- Team experiments with alternative formats
  (e.g. Lean Coffee, Six Thinking Hats, etc.)

 vimeopro.com/leandog/retrospectives

"Agile Retrospectives: Making Good Teams Great"
By Esther Derby & Diana Larsen

Velocity

Velocity is a simple, yet powerful method to consistently measure and track the rate a team delivers business value in each iteration. It is measured by counting the completed cards from the iteration that is ending. Then the velocity is used to determine and plan upcoming sprints/iterations and estimate time of completion.

Essential

- Must be measured
- If a card is not finished within a sprint/iteration, the card and points are carried to the next sprint/iteration
- Never take partial credit, don't split points across sprints/iterations; "not done" means zero points in the iteration even if only one hour of work is required to finish
- The team's previous velocity is used as the first guess of a future velocity
- Well understood by the whole team: "What was your velocity for the last sprint/iteration?"
- Managers look at burn up charts, not velocity
- Point method must be consistent within the team; does not have to be consistent across the teams
- Velocity adjusted based on holidays and large team absences

When a team and their environment are healthy, velocity should stabilize after 3-6 iterations to a predictable number range. A highly volatile velocity 5 or 6 iterations is an indicator that the dynamics around or within the team has not stabilized and warrants further inspection and adaptation.

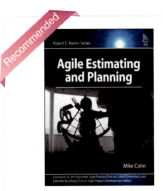

"Agile Estimating & Planning"
By Mike Cohn

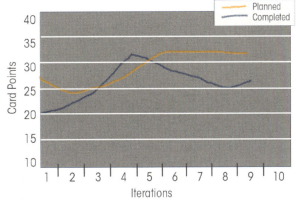

Velocity is the amount of work the team can get completed in one sprint/iteration

 vimeopro.com/leandog/velocity

Roadblocks

A roadblock is an obstacle that is standing in the way of the team. Management should be aware of roadblocks early so they are quickly resolved and the rest of the card can be completed in a timely manner.

Essential

- Displayed on a wall in each team area
- Roadblocks are prioritized and completed in order
- Reviewed at end of each iteration/sprint
- When in progress, there should be an owner on the card
- Are declared during stand up

Advanced

- Date on the card denotes roadblock's inception
- Break roadblocks into columns of progress
- Create an escalation process for roadblocks in the event someone needs help
- Purpose of roadblock wall is clearly defined
- Senior management understands that roadblocks exist and where to find them

"Succeeding with Agile: Software Development Using Scrum"
By Mike Cohn

 vimeopro.com/leandog/roadblocks

Chapter 6

Quality Assurance

In this chapter
- Quality Assurance Role
- Exploratory Testing
- Automated Regression Testing
- Acceptance Test Driven Development

Quality Assurance Role

A Quality Assurance role is one where team members are responsible for inspecting and/or validating the product delivered both within the context of a story and as a whole.

Essential

- Continually improve the tests with refactoring (including data)
- Work with the product owner and developer to establish a plan for providing business value
- Understand the business intent of the story card which help define tests to measure the effectiveness of the story implementation
- Collect and organize story tests into an automated test suite that becomes the regression test
- Run and define exploratory tests and communicates results

Advanced

- Undertake testing craftsmanship to help maintain development speed, quality, and efficiency
- Commit to be one of the "Three Amigos" / "Fantastic Four", with excellent collaboration between product owner and developers
- Assist with defining features and specifications with Acceptance Test Driven Development (ATDD)
- Automate ATDD tests
- Pair with a fellow team members to ensure someone else knows that section of the application, and hold each other to high levels of test quality

"Agile Testing: practical Guide Testers and Agile Teams"
By Lisa Crispin & Janet Gregory

Exploratory Testing

Exploratory Testing is a method of questioning and learning about the product as you design and execute tests, as opposed to following a predefined script. This is considered a mode of simultaneous learning, test design and test execution that values the tester as a critical part of the test process.

Essential

- Manual tests that occur during and after the story is developed
- Used to catch the edge cases that aren't caught in automation
- Integral part of the quality strategy for a team or a project
- Involves the tester before the story card is implemented and throughout delivery of the story card

Advanced

- Is never "done"
- Is usually executed against a "charter"
- May be constrained to a time-boxed session between 30 and 120 minutes

vimeopro.com/leandog/exploratory-testing

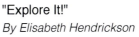
"Explore It!"
By Elisabeth Hendrickson

Automated Regression Testing

Automated Regression Testing is a testing process focused on detecting defects introduced into the software at the earliest possible opportunity while eliminating repetitive manual labor. Automated Regression Testing uses a comprehensive suite of automated tests to confirm the proper operation of each feature in the application, and notifies the team if one or more features of the software is not operating correctly.

Essential

- An iterative activity to build up a regression test suite by creating tests prior to writing code
- Tests are executed every time code is checked into the code repository, resulting in immediate feedback on the health of the overall code base
- Scripts are created for regression testing
- Automated tools run the scripts for regression testing
- Automated testing with duplicable test data generation
- Test entire application, both new and existing functionality, at least once per sprint/iteration
- In order to keep up with development efforts, regression testing must be automated
- Most development efforts are on existing applications. If you do not have great test coverage, where do you start?
    - With buggy or trouble areas
    - If no trouble areas, then start with the critical application areas
    - Any new functionality

Advanced

- See the Acceptance Test Driven Development process for more guidance on improving the effectiveness and efficiency of regression testing

"Agile Testing: practical Guide Testers and Agile Teams"
By Lisa Crispin & Janet Gregory

What is "ility" Testing?
Testing concerned with qualities such as security, maintainability, interoperability, compatibility, reliability, and installability[1].
Learn More in "Agile Testing" by Lisa Crsipin

 vimeopro.com/leandog/automated-regression-testing

1 "Agile Testing: practical Guide Testers and Agile Teams" By Lisa Crispin & Janet Gregory

Acceptance Test Driven Development

Acceptance Test Driven Development (ATDD) is a practice in which the team discusses the acceptance criteria, then creates a set of clear acceptance tests before development begins. It ensures that the team has a shared understanding of what is being developed. It requires a significant shift in how the team members interact with each other. The transition to ATDD can be a challenge, but the payback is significant.

Essential

- Requirements are captured as combinations of free-form specification and Gherkin scenarios that describe how the system should behave when completed. These scenarios become the Acceptance Tests
- Just prior to the development of a story, the product owner, tester and developer meet to refine and add any missing Acceptance Tests. We call this a "Three Amigos" meeting
- Automation of the Acceptance Tests must be completed prior to the completion of development
- Developer focuses on making the Acceptance Tests pass. Together with the tester, their focus throughout this effort is to prevent defects
- Story is functionally complete once all Acceptance Tests pass
- Acceptance Tests run continuously to act as a regression test
- The definition of "done" must be clear

Advanced

- Tester automates Acceptance Tests at same time as the developer writes code. They are in constant collaboration during this effort

```
Feature: Checkout out after selecting a puppy

  In order to complete my online adoption
  as a customer of the puppy adoption site
  I want to be able to checkout by providing necessary information

  It is important to capture the necessary information we require to
  process the adoption.  We need to create a screen that captures the
  name, address, email address and payment type of the customer.

  Scenario: Name is a required field
    Given I am on the puppy adoption site
    When I adopt a puppy leaving the name field blank
    Then I should see the error message "Name can't be blank"

  Scenario: Thank you message should be displayed when adoption completed
    Given I am on the puppy adoption site
    When I complete the adoption of a puppy
    Then I should see "Thank you for adopting a puppy!"
```

Acceptance Test Driven Development

Acceptance Test Driven Development Process

ATDD moves quality from defect detection as the last stage in the process to defect prevention through better communication and a collective understanding from the start.

Step 1: A backlog is produced based on functional requirements

BACKLOG - A list of stories to be delivered.

Step 2: Product Owner, Quality Assurance, and Developer collaborate to review the specification, make any necessary adjustments and add missing requirements and edge cases.

Executable Specifications - Scenarios are captured to ensure an accurate understanding of a feature.

RED Light: There is a red light between steps 2 and 3 because the code has yet to be written.

Step 4: The story is deemed functionally complete when all acceptance tests pass and and they have been added to the regression suite.

DELIVERABLE - A story that is ready for delivery to the customer.

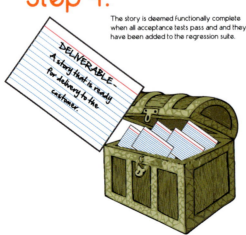

GREEN Light: There is a green light between steps 3 and 4 because the code has passed the tests.

Step 3: QA automates the specifications, while the the DEV implements the features.

IMPLEMENT - Building the specified feature.

Acceptance Test Driven Development

Current Process

Software development has come a long way, but the focus remains on project management and developer practices. For most, Quality Assurance (QA) is still about defect detection instead of defect prevention.

Step 1

The product owner writes initial requirements in the form of specifications and scenarios. Other supplemental artifacts such as low-fidelity prototypes and possible wireframes are acceptable, but the core functional requirements must be captured in scenarios.

Step 2

Just prior to story development, the product owner, tester and developer (Three Amigos) and UX if available (Fantastic Four) meet to review and finalize the scenarios. At this time, the tester typically introduces edge cases that were absent from original scenarios. The developer can also take this opportunity to discuss other possibilities and alternatives that might simplify the delivery. At the end of this meeting, the product owner agrees that the story is complete once scenarios pass.

Step 3

The developer and tester focus on preventing defects and making all scenarios pass. Ideally, the tester automates the scenarios at the same time the developer is writing code. Once all scenarios are automated, the tester can initiate exploratory testing on application and continue to provide feedback to the developer. This collaboration continues until all scenarios pass and both parties feel they have tested all aspects of the story.

ATDD Poster
LeanDog.com/free/attdposter.pdf

vimeopro.com/leandog/atdd

"Cucumber & Cheese:
A Testers Workshop"
By Jeff Morgan

Chapter 7

Developer

In this chapter
- Developer Role
- Collective Code Ownership
- Continuous Integration
- Simple & Evolutionary Design
- Paired Programming (Pairing)
- Test Driven Development
- Technical Debt
- Spikes

Developer Role

A developer is responsible for creating high-quality working code that meets the expectations of the product owner.

Essential

- Understands the business intent of the story card
- Works with the product owner and tester to come up with an approach on how to provide the value
- Save both test and code in a repository
- Build code to satisfy the tests and conditions of the story
- Write and code with the purpose of clearly communicating the intent to the next developer that will look at the code, and be satisfied that what you have coded is ready for production use
- Build tests that measure whether or not the implementation is working
- Continually improve the test and code base with refactoring
- Pair with a fellow developer to ensure someone else knows this section of the application, and hold each other to high levels of design and code quality

Advanced

- Undertake software craftsmanship to help maintain development speed, quality and efficiency
- Commit to be one of the "Three Amigos"/ "Fantastic Four" and encourage collaboration between product owner and quality assurance
- Build code to get acceptance tests to pass (ATDD - Acceptance Test Driven Development)

"Clean Code: A Handbook of Agile Software Craftmanship"
By Robert C. Martin

Collective Code Ownership

Collective Code Ownership is a practice where all team members share responsibility for code quality. It also allows each developer to change any piece of the code at any time. Collective Code Ownership also helps to eliminate "specialization", as everyone is expected to fix problems when they are discovered.

Essential

- All developers are responsible for the code; everyone has the ability to change the code
- Developers commit to writing outstanding new code from the start, instead of doing a half-hearted job and expecting someone else to fix the mistakes
- Check egos at the door
- Works best when coupled with Paired Programming and Test Driven Development
- Eliminate knowledge silos by encouraging developers to work in unfamiliar areas of code

Collective Code Ownership

We are members of a community that owns the code

Anyone can modify any code at any time
Team has a single style guide and coding standard
Original authorship is immaterial
Plentiful automated tests increase confidence and safety

 vimeopro.com/leandog/collective-code-ownership

"Practices of an Agile Developer"
By Venkat Subromanian & Andy Hunt

Continuous Integration

Continuous Integration is the practice of ensuring all code changes are compatible with the existing shared codebase by assimilating each change into the codebase as soon as possible after a developer submits the change. The entire system is tested in order to confirm the health of the code and verify that the changes made are compatible with the shared codebase. Testing is performed using an automated, scripted process known as "the build".

Essential
- System is built and all unit tests run at least once a day
- The entire build and test run takes no more than ten minutes
- Team is notified whenever a build fails
- Fixing a broken build is the team's highest priority

Advanced
- A system is built and all tests are run every time a developer checks in code
- Visual indicators in the room that show the build status

"Jenkins Continuous Integration Cookbook"
By Alan Berg

"Continuous Integration: Improving Software Quality and Reducing Risk"
By Paul M. Duvall

 vimeopro.com/leandog/continuous-integration

Simple & Evolutionary Design

Simple & Evolutionary design is a system which minimizes the amount of up-front design done before coding begins. Instead, the design of the system grows as it develops, emphasizing simple architectures and designs that provide adaptability to change. Simple designs also allow teams to have increased velocity as they spend more time providing customer value.

Essential

- "Simple is best" approach to software design where refactoring is an integral part of the code simplification process
- Believes in doing "the simplest thing that works"
- Avoid building unnecessary architecture
- Design is done just in time and evolves with the app
- Spikes are used to mitigate risk in design or investigate a new domain

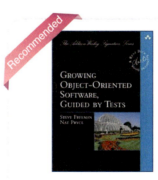

"Growing Object-Oriented Software guided by tests"
By Steve Freeman

 vimeopro.com/leandog/simple-and-evolutionary-design

Paired Programming (Pairing)

Paired Programming is the technique of joining two team members at one computer. With two minds in constant collaboration, paired programming encourages sharing knowledge and catching bugs early by continual code review. The knowledge moves across the team more quickly and ensures that the best practices are followed.

Essential

- All code is produced by a pair of developers working together on one story at one workstation
- It's encouraged for all roles to pair with anyone, anytime - switching every few hours is optimal
- Pairs change frequently, and very few knowledge silos exist
- No coding without a pair partner
- Don't underestimate good hygiene
- Environment supports pairing: desks are easy to access, office doesn't have obstacles or obstructions
- Developers do not have their backs to the team, they sit beside or across from each other

Advanced

- Frequent pair switching - switch pairs every 2-4 hours
- Remote Pairing
- Pairs use focusing techniques (e.g. Pomodoro) to stay on task

"The Art of Agile Development"
By James Shore

Recommended article:

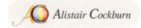

"The Cost & Benefits of Pair Programming"
By Alistair Cockburn

 vimeopro.com/leandog/paired-programming

Test Driven Development

Test Driven Development is a software development technique where developers write a test prior to any new application code and use short development cycles to design the product. There are three stages: (1) Write a failing test, (2) Write code to make it pass, (3) Refactor and continue cycle until the developers cannot think of any more tests. Using TDD results in fewer defects, and provides a fast feedback loop, allowing for fearless refactoring of the system.

Essential

- Tests are written prior to any code
- TDD workflow:
    - Write a failing test
    - Write code to make the test pass
    - Refactor and continue cycle until the system fulfills all required functionality and satisfies all known use cases
- Forces testable designs/architectures
- Produces clean code
- Tests to provide a safety net as application design evolves

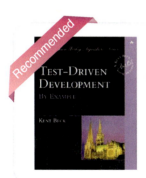

"Test Driven Development: By Example"
By Kent Beck

vimeopro.com/leandog/tdd

Technical Debt

Technical Debt is the gap between the right solution and the solution that currently exists. As technical debt accrues, the more difficult it becomes to reconcile the differences and deliver what is needed. Technical debt can be incurred as a strategic initiative, but needs to be repaid within only a few iterations.

Essential

- Clean code
- Good test coverage
- A learning objective
- Payback plan
- A truly informed product owner

Advanced

- Technical debt is tracked / acknowledged / disclosed
- Technical debt is continuously minimized

	Reckless	Prudent
Deliberate	"We don't have time for design"	"We must ship now and deal with consequences"
Inadvertent	"What's Layering?"	"Now we know how we should have done it"

"Working Effectively with Legacy Code"
By Michael Feathers

 vimeopro.com/leandog/technical-debt

Spikes

A Spike is a time-boxed experimental story card that is included in the iteration cycle to determine an estimate, but stops short of completing the story. Spikes are an excellent way to try out something quickly, and are usually a few hours to a couple days in length.

Essential
- Time-boxed
- Few in number
- A learning / discovery objective
- Code produced should be thrown away
- Results should be communicated back to the team and product owner along with demos
- Pulled forward in the release plan to reduce risk
- Played with enough leeway to adapt the plan
- Incorporate spikes into planning
- Estimate the spike like anything else

"The Art of Agile Development"
By James Shore

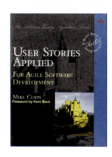

"User Stories Applied: For Agile Software Development"
By Mike Cohn

vimeopro.com/leandog/spikes

80

Chapter 8

Product Owner

In this chapter
- Product Owner Role
- Value Stream Mapping
- Demand Management
- Product Backlog
- Release Planning

Product Owner Role

The product owner represents the stakeholders and acts as the voice of the customer. They are accountable for ensuring that the team delivers value to the business. The product owner writes customer-centric items (typically user stories), prioritizes them, and adds them to the product backlog. Scrum teams should have one product owner, and while they may also be a member of the development team, it is recommended that this role not be combined with that of scrum master.

Essential

- Decides what will be built and in which order
- Defines the features of the product or desired outcomes of the project
- Orders the product backlog to best achieve goals and missions
- Prioritizes features and outcomes according to market value
- Facilitates release planning ceremony with iteration manager
- Adjusts features, outcomes and priority as needed
- Accepts or rejects work results

"Agile Product Management with Scrum: Creating Products that Customers Love"
By Roman Pichler

 vimeopro.com/leandog/product-owner-role

Agile Project Management with Scrum, Ken Schwaber

Value Stream Mapping

Value stream mapping is a type of flow chart used to design and analyze the flow of information needed to bring a product to the customer. Mapping allows you to discover waste, then construct a plan to eliminate it.

Essential

- Flow of activities begins with the customer's need and ends when the need is satisfied
- Identify the target product, product family or service
- Draw a current state value stream map illustrating current steps, delays and information flows required to deliver the target product
- Assess the current state value stream map in terms of creating flow and eliminating waste
- Draw a future state value stream map

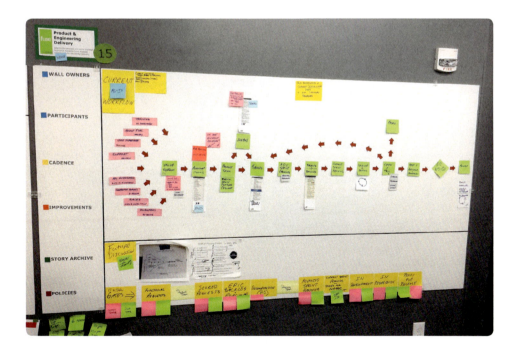

 vimeopro.com/leandog/value-stream-mapping

83

Demand Management

Demand Management helps organizations deliver the most value from their capacity by adopting continuous portfolio alignment, incorporating pull-based thinking, and limiting work in progress (WIP).

Essential

- Regular User Summits bring all users together in order by value to discuss their goals
- Project demand funnel is visible to team
- Cards are ordered by highest value
- Everyone understands concept of Minimal Marketable Feature (MMF) or Minimal Usable Feature (MUF)

Advanced

- Customer personas are present and considered
- Story Mapping technique is used and understood by everyone

See the Whole - Lean Software Development
Standard Workflow: From Idea to Production

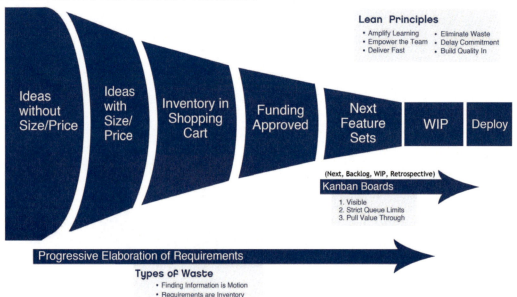

 vimeopro.com/leandog/demand-management

84

Product Backlog

The Product Backlog is a high-level list of all potential features prioritized by business value for the customer.

Essential

- Just enough product backlog to create product without unnecessary features
- Must be visible
- Uses concept of Minimal Marketable Feature Sets (MMFS)
- Must prioritize and organize backlog by business value
- Backlog is regularly reviewed and maintained
- Not a requirements list
- Team and Customer collaborate on prioritization, to ensure that technical complexity, duration, and cost of features are understood to the extent that they impact business value
- Customer has final decision authority around prioritization of features.

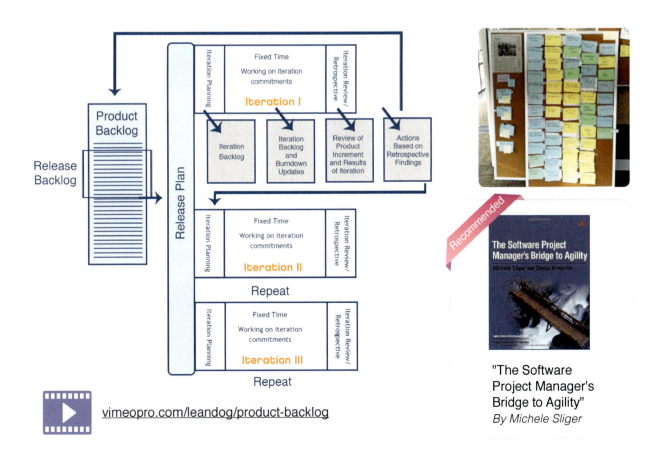

vimeopro.com/leandog/product-backlog

"The Software Project Manager's Bridge to Agility"
By Michele Sliger

Michele Sliger and Stacia Broderick, "The Software Project Manager's Bridge to Agility"

Release Planning

A Release Plan is an evolving roadmap that sets delivery goals for high-level feature sets. It will provide the team with an overview of the release and what is required to make the release a success. The plan should include the key features, goals, responsibilities, and risks.

Essential

- Core team, business owner, and supporting roles drive out product features, details, and stories for release; anything not deemed part of the release will either be out of scope, or moved to a future release
- Planning the next release is a joint effort between business partners and team
- Release plans map out several iterations to package releases and maximize business value
- Spikes are used to identify and mitigate risk, risk is pulled forward
- Produce burn up/down charts
- Lay out cards in order of feature importance
- Team agrees to a planning velocity which is used to create the Release Plan

Advanced

- Release Planning is a continuous activity for regularly scheduled releases
- Suggest a rolling release planning window
- Suggest a separate Release Planning Meeting with product owners to prioritize next set of features to work on for upcoming releases

The team should review plan and ask the following Questions:
- Is there enough work for all pairs?
- Are any pairs stepping on others?
- Are highest risk cards being played first?
- Are the most valuable features coming out first?
- Are there any dependencies which are missing?

"Product Release Planning: Methods, Tools and Applications"
By Guenther Ruhe

vimeopro.com/leandog/release-planning

Chapter 9

User Experience

In this chapter
- User Experience Designer
- Personas
- Story Mapping
- Low-Fidelity Prototyping

User Experience Designer

The User Experience (UX) Designer(s) are responsible for defining, designing and testing the experiences and interactions that users of the system engage with. UX is a broad spectrum of skills that include information architecture, user research, data analysis, content strategy, visual design and usability. All of these elements come together to craft a measurable user experience.

Essential

- Start with the problem and business objective
- Follow the 80/20 rule by focusing on the core functionality, or "happy path"
- Stay one step ahead of the team, before development work begins
- Do just enough design
- Iterate your designs (refactoring is to be expected)
- Test and validate with users
- Communicate with your team
- Define success metrics

Advanced

- Stay 1-2 sprints/iterations ahead of development
- Design spikes
- Cross-functional pairing
- Facilitate ideation sessions and encourage the team to participate
- Co-located to be part of the team
- Define styles and patterns for common elements early in the process
- Visualize the workflow or interactions
- UX design reviews

"Universal Methods of Design: 100 Ways to Research Complex Problems, Develop Innovative Ideas, and Design Effective Solutions"
By Bruce Hanington & Bella Martin

"Agile Experience: A Digital Designer's Guide to Agile, Lean, and Continuous Improvement"
By Lindsay Ratcliffe & Marc McNeill

Picture source: Peter Morville of Semantic Studios put together this concept of the UX Honeycomb in 2004

Personas

Personas are profiles of the customers who will be using your product. They are an important tool that helps reduce waste by ensuring all features are necessary. Personas typically include: behavior and usage patterns, goals and motives, knowledge or skills, and sometimes the person's role and demographic. Personas are not made-up, but researched thoroughly. The goal is to define the target audience you are designing the system for.

Essential:

- Customer base is depicted visually
- Personas are based on a subset of the customer profile
- Understand your customer clearly
- Provide an instance of user types
- Take scenarios from personas
- Avoid mirror personas and elastic users
- Design each part of the interface for just one persona
- Should "wiggle" under the pressure of development
- No more than three primary personas for the entire system
- Describe current situation of customer profile, describe goals, needs of the profile, and how will application being created add value to person

Linda Cole, Home Buyer:

Goals:
- Move into a bigger house
- Better life for her kids than she had

Situation:
- 34 years old
- Current home not large enough
- Drives kids to school each morning

Value:
- Our web app will show her the availability of homes in the area.
- App allows user to access information about available homes

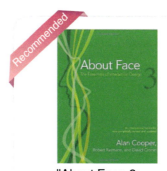

"About Face 3: The Essentials of Interaction Design"
By David Cronin, Robert Relmann, Alan Cooper

 vimeopro.com/leandog/personas

Page source: Jeff Patton, http://www.agileweboperations.com/pragmatic-personas-concrete-examples-of-your-users

89

Story Mapping

Story mapping is the highest level in the ideation process and should be completed first. It includes every feature you want in your product. A story map is categorized by size, then grouped together by features that are linked or related.

Essential

- Early stage of progressive elaboration
- Team uses note cards to depict the features and their flow in the system
- Start at the Epic level and continue on down into user stories, then into features
- Features are organized by value order
- Discovery and Prioritization
- Used early on, not an ongoing practice
- Technique can be applied to reverse engineer an application
- A good tool for getting people to think through what they are asking for

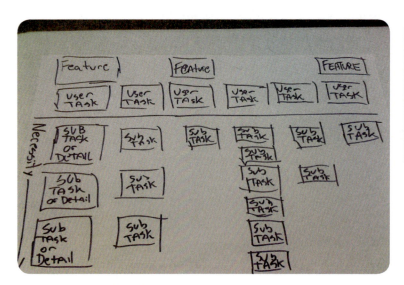

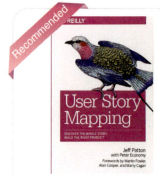

"User Story Mapping: Discover the Whole Story, Build the Right Product"
By Jeff Patton

 vimeopro.com/leandog/story-mapping

Low-Fidelity Prototyping

Low-Fidelity Prototyping is a tool used to create a mock-up that is quick and incomplete, but has the characteristics of the target product. It's simple and requires minimal effort to quickly produce the prototype and test broad concepts.

Essential:
- Initial version of user interface is created manually
- Rapid iterations and prototypes with team members
- Build the software and encourage interaction

Advanced:
- Creation of storyboards that represent a larger portion of the project
- Lightweight, no tools, fast

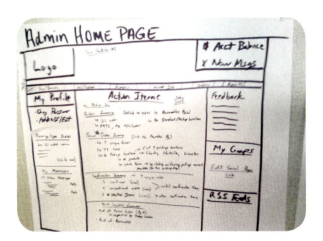
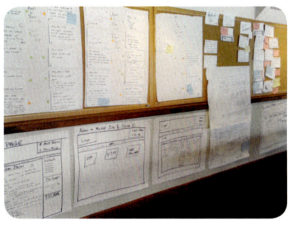

"Sketching User Experiences: Getting the Design Right and the Right Design"
By Bill Buxton

 vimeopro.com/leandog/low-fidelity-prototyping

91

Appendix

Recommended Reading List

The LeanDog team has a recommended reading list detailing which books are best for the Business Analyst, Quality Assurance, Management, Developers, Scrum Masters, and Product Owners. Each of these have helped us further our knowledge of practicing Agile in not only our software development, but our company as a whole.

Recommended For:

Business Analyst	BA
Quality Assurance	QA
Management	MGMT
Developer	DEV
Scrum Master	SM
Product Owner	PO
User Experience	UX

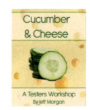

"Cucumber & Cheese: A Testers Workshop"
By Jeff Morgan

QA DEV

"Agile Retrospectives: Making Good Teams Great"
By Esther Derby & Diana Larsen

BA PO

"Agile Project Management: Creating Innovative Products"
By Jim Highsmith

BA MGMT PO

"An Agile Adoption and Transformation Survival Guide"
By Michael Sahota

Everyone

"Agile Estimating and Planning"
By Mike Cohn

SM

"Apprenticeship Patterns: Guidance for the Aspiring Software Craftsman"
By Dave Hoover & Adewale Oshineye

BA QA PO

"The Art of Agile Development"
By James Shore & Chromatic

BA QA DEV SM PO UX

"Agile Testing: A Practical Guide for Testers and Agile Teams"
By Lisa Crispin & Janet Gregory

QA DEV

"The Agile Samuai: How Agile Masters Deliver Great Software"
By Jonathan Rasmusson

QA DEV SM PO UX

"Extreme Programming Explained: Embrace Change"
By Ken Beck, Cynthia Andres

QA DEV

"Everyday Scripting with Ruby: for Teams, Testers, and You"
By Brian Marick

QA DEV

"Clean Code: A Handbook of Agile Software Craftsmanship"
By Robert C Martin

DEV

"The Clean Coder: A Code of Conduct for Professional Programmers"
By Robert C. Martin

QA DEV

Recommended Reading List

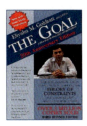

"The Goal"
By Eiyahu M. Goldratt

MGMT

"Hacking Vim 7.2"
By Kim Schulz

DEV

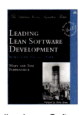

"Leading Lean Software Development: Results are Not the Point"
By Mary Poppendieck & Tom Poppendieck   MGMT

"Management 3.0: Leading Agile Developers, Developing Agile Leaders"
By Jurgen Appelo

MGMT   PO   SM

"Metaprogramming Ruby: Program Like the Ruby Pros"
By Paolo Perotta

DEV

"The Passionate Programmer: Creating a Remarkable Career in Software Development"
By Chad Fowler   DEV

"Pragmatic Guide to Git"
By Travis Swicegood

DEV

"The Pragmatic Programmer: From Journeyman to Master"
By Andrew Hunt & David Thomas

QA   DEV

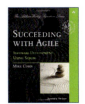

"Succeeding with Agile: Software Development using Scrum"
By Mike Cohn

BA   MGMT   DEV   SM   PO   UX

"User Stories Applied: For Agile Software Development"
By Mike Cohn

DEV

"The Software Project Managers: Bridge to Agility"
By Michele Sliger & Stacia Broderick

BA   PO

"Specfication by example"
By Gojko Adzic

DEV

"Product Release Planning: Methods, Tools and Applications"
By Guenther Ruhe

BA   PO   SM   DEV   UX

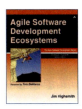

"Agile Software Development Ecosystems"
By Jim Highsmith

BA   DEV

"Sketching User Experiences: Getting the Design Right and the Right Design"
By Bill Buxton   UX

"About Face 3: The Essentials of Interaction Design"
By David Cronin, Robert Relmann, Alan Cooper   UX

95

Recommended Reading List

"Kanban: Successful Evolutionary Change for your Technology Business"
By David J Anderson

BA DEV SM PO UX

"Agile Experience: A Digital Designer's Guide to Agile, Lean, and Continuous Improvement" *By Lindsay Ratcliffe & Marc McNeill*

UX

"Growing Object-Oriented Software guided by tests"
By Steve Freeman

QA DEV

"Agile Software Development: The Cooperative Game"
By Alistair Cockburn

BA DEV SM PO UX

"Six Thinking Hats"
By Edward de Bono

MGMT

"Practices of an Agile Developer"
By Venkat Subramaniam and Andy Hunt

DEV

"Test Driven Development: By Example"
By Kent Beck

QA DEV

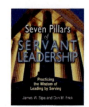

"Seven Pillars of Servant Leadership: Practicing the Wisdom of Leading by Serving"
By James W. Sipe & Don M. Frick

MGMT

"Continuous Integration: Improving Software Quality and Reducing Risk"
By Paul M. Duvall

DEV

"Jenkins Continuous Integration Cookbook"
By Alan Berg

DEV

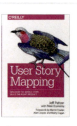

"User Story Mapping: Discover the Whole Story, Build the Right Product"
By Jeff Patton

BA QA SM PO UX

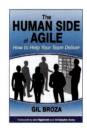

"The Human Side of Agile"
By Gil Broza

BA MGMT SM PO

"100 Ways to Research Complex Problems, Develop Innovative Ideas, and Design Effective Solutions" *By Bruce Hanington & Bella Martin*

UX

"Explore It!: Reduce Risk and Increase Confidence with Exploratory Testing"
By Elisabeth Hendrickson

QA

"Agile Product Management with Scrum: Creating Products that Customers Love"
By Roman Pichler

BA SM PO

"Collaboration: How Leaders Avoid the Traps, Create Unity, and Reap Big Results"
By Morten Hansen

BA MGMT PO UX

96

Additional Downloads

Bring best practices into your world today with these tools you can use to streamline product development and delivery.

Posters & Signs you can print:

- Agile Signs & Posters
- Agile Principles Poster
- Agile Manifesto Poster
- Information Radiators & Wall Signs

Available at LeanDog.com/downloads

Download Our App
LeanDog Agile Tools

Use our mobile collaboration cards to help you estimate, plan, and gain consensus.

Cards included:
- Six Thinking Hats
- Collaboration 8
- Fist to Five
- T-Shirt Sizing

About this Author

LeanDog is redefining smart design and delivery; guiding the path to transformation and developing software solutions to change lives.

We began in 2008 with one simple goal: Put together 20 brilliant minds, and have a blast creating groundbreaking software. We've found a lot more than 20 great minds since then. Our skill set has grown to include expert coaching, training and embedded collaboration, along with our thriving design and delivery studio.

LeanDog offers a fine-tuned approach to product development that cuts through barriers and ensures a focus on delivering the greatest value to the business. And we know that communication is everything. That's why we work hard to promote the kind of collaboration that transforms cultures and brings ideas to market faster.

We're out there daily sharing these insights with the world – Lean, Agile and a pocketful of other philosophies that drive quality. And we practice what we teach every day in our software development studio.

We chose a 120-year old boat as our headquarters to inspire greatness – in ourselves, our community and in our clients. As soon as you step on our boat, you realize that we think, act, work, and do things differently. We hope to inspire you to continually learn and grow with us.

Connect with us:
LeanDog.com • 216.236.4705 • info@leandog.com

Made in the USA
Middletown, DE
04 September 2016